The Ford Engineering Laboratory

A Historical View

Beth Ann Dalrymple

M. T. Publishing Company, Inc.™

P.O. Box 6802
Evansville, Indiana 47719-6802
www.mtpublishing.com

Copyright © 2016
Ford Motor Company
All rights reserved.

Graphic Designer: Raven Fields

Library of Congress Control Number: 2016921239

ISBN: 978-1-945306-48-8

Printed in the United States of America

"The farther you look back the farther you can look ahead."

— Henry Ford

Introduction

When this revolutionary building first opened more than 90 years ago, great minds would pass through its doors pursuing dreams that helped push forward the interests of mankind. The Ford Engineering Laboratory's Romanesque style symbolizes a passion to advance innovation and mobility, a passion that was in play when the building was built in 1924 and that endures today in the very DNA of Ford Motor Company. I am proud that what once held the inspirational minds of yesterday, today houses great talent working to ensure a better world for the future. The Ford Engineering Laboratory is a true treasure.

— Edsel B. Ford, II

The Ford Engineering Laboratory during construction in early 1924.

Foreword

History is a key to the future. Revisiting an institution's achievements and places of operation allows a person to glance at the foundation that brought about transformation and accomplishment. Ford Motor Company and its founder Henry Ford helped reshape the way the world worked and lived. Many of the ideas for the changes the company helped to institute came directly from the people's minds at the Ford Engineering Laboratory. This collection of photographs and text invites the reader to step back in time to an era of dramatic innovation.

— *Robert C. Kreipke*
Ford Motor Company Historian

The interior of the Ford Engineering Laboratory during construction in early 1924.

The Ford Engineering Laboratory

Henry Ford, the man who put Detroit and the world on wheels, together with Albert Kahn, who was often referred to as the man who built Detroit, would design and build a state of the art design and engineering facility in Dearborn, Michigan. This facility is known as the Ford Engineering Laboratory (FEL) and was completed in 1924.

It was a modern marvel of architectural beauty and simplicity; a first of its kind as a comprehensive design and engineering facility. The Ford Engineering Laboratory would house the largest hard rock maple wood floor in the world at 160,000 square feet. The ceilings would contain over 64,000 square feet of glass, allowing unlimited natural light into the wide-open design space. This space would include everything necessary to design and engineer vehicles, and much more.

This new facility would have space for engine design, dynamometers, wood pattern making, a machine shop, an electrical lab, a chemical lab, clay modeling, body engineering & styling, blue printing, a photography lab, publishing, radio communications, and even a ballroom for dancing.

Within this book lies the incredible 90-year history, and legacy of the Ford Engineering Laboratory and its inhabitants told through a photographer's lens. Each turn of a page delves deeper into the progress, and people-driven world of Ford automobile design & engineering. All the individuals' past and present who have worked within these walls continue to pave the way for all mankind to go further.

— Beth Ann Dalrymple

Acknowledgements

I want to thank Kevin Layden for asking me to put together a photo book of the Ford Engineering Laboratory as a special project, which has led to this book. I also wish to thank Bob Kriepke, the Ford Motor Company Historian, for sharing his stories and his encouragement. I want to thank Linda Skolarus for all her help and encouragement. Lastly this book would not have been as lovely without Raven Fields one of the most talented graphic designers I could have just happened upon. Thank you all for your talent, your wealth of knowledge and your friendship.

—Beth Ann Dalrymple

Ford Motor Company Archives

Ford Photographic

Brian Wybenga

Charlotte Bodak

Staff at the Benson Ford Research Center

Neeley Edelman

Jamie Myler

Janine McFadden

Gael Sandoval

Ashley Allison

Pam Stith

Thomas Miller

Elizabeth Munger

Nardina Mein

Mike Imirie

This book is dedicated to Pamela J. Fazzini, a dear childhood friend of mine who lost her battle with Juvenile Diabetes at the age of 34.

Engineering Laboratory and Airport
Ford Motor Company

A postcard from 1926 showing an aerial view of the Ford Engineering Laboratory and airport prior to the creation of the Edison Institute Museum & Historical Greenfield Village (The Henry Ford).

Ford Engineering Laboratory
Dearborn, Michigan 1930

1930 aerial view of the Ford Engineering Laboratory and the Edison Institute Museum & Historical Greenfield Village.

The Ford Engineering Laboratory, 2015.

MANKIND PASSES FROM THE OLD TO THE NEW ON A HUMAN BRIDGE FORMED BY THOSE WHO LABOR IN THE THREE PRINCIPAL ARTS - AGRICULTURE -- MANUFACTURE -- - TRANSPORTATION -

The very detailed ornamental reliefs on the façade of the Ford Engineering Laboratory are known as Beaux-Art reliefs and were very popular on industrial buildings and private homes in the United States from the mid 1890's to 1930. This very ornate style of art was taught in Paris at the turn of the century. These reliefs are common in ancient Greek and Roman architecture both inside and outside of buildings and temples; they often tell a narrative about the people or the structure.

This beautiful relief is above the front entrance of the building. The male and female figures are holding a Ford Sedan and a Fordson tractor representing transportation, manufacturing, and agriculture.

13

The Ford Engineering Laboratory lobby, circa 2007.

The photo to the left shows intricate details of the bronze ornamental vestibule in the lobby.

Mahogany Row facing north, circa 1936.

Mahogany Row facing south, circa 2015.

This is often referred to as Mahogany Row because of the beautiful coloring of the wood panels; however, the wood is actually walnut.

Marble staircase, circa 2007.

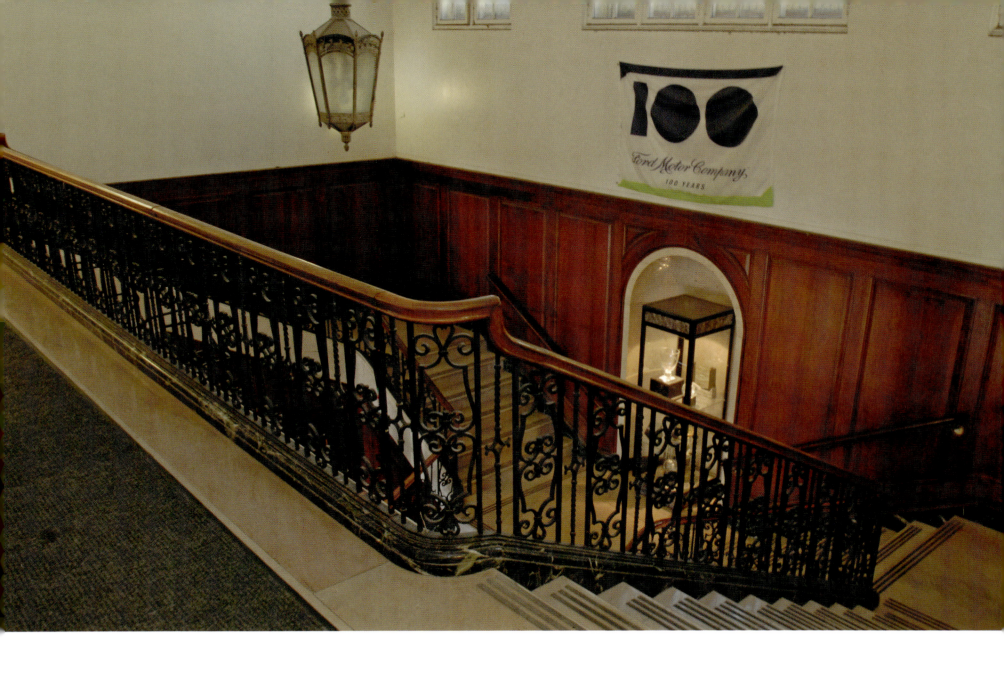

This photo was taken from the second floor offices looking down on the marble staircase in 2007.

Henry and Edsel Ford with several of their executives at the north end of FEL, 1933.

Henry and Edsel Ford looking at a model of the Rouge Complex, in the Ford Engineering Laboratory in the 1920's.

Edsel Ford's office in the Ford Engineering Laboratory, circa 1924.

Henry Ford's office in the Ford Engineering Laboratory, circa 1924.

Above is the composing room of the Dearborn Publishing Company at the Ford Engineering Laboratory, in 1925. Editorial offices and printing for the Dearborn Independent, Ford News, and the D.T.I. Railroad News were located in the building.

Ar. X-3 prototype engine block, circa 1926.

The drafting room in the Ford Engineering Laboratory, circa 1928.

Power Plant construction, circa 1930.

Henry Ford sitting in the Ford Engineering Laboratory, notice the museum is in the background, undated.

Henry Ford, Ernest Liebold and others, undated.

A 1932 Ford V8 Engine.

Edsel Ford, Henry Ford, Charles Sorenson, and other Ford Motor Company executives shown at lunch in the Executive Dining Room at the Ford Engineering Laboratory in 1933.

Edsel Ford and Henry Ford at the Ford Engineering Laboratory, circa 1935.

Rare rear view photo of the Ford Engineering Laboratory and powerhouse taken from the village, circa 1936. Radio operators inside the FEL communicated with the trains and ships bringing in materials to Ford Motor Company.

Henry Ford's love of dancing prompted him to put in a dance room at the Ford Engineering Laboratory. Mr. Ford felt that old-fashioned dancing taught proper social skills. Friday evening dances were held here for Ford executives. Shown here, in the dance room of the Ford Engineering Laboratory, are students most likely from the Edison Institute School, circa 1936.

Henry Ford celebrated his 74th birthday at the Ford Engineering Laboratory with chemist, Robert Boyer, in 1937. Boyer worked to turn soy beans into paint and plastic parts.

Robert Boyer and Henry Ford with the "Soybean Car", which was actually a plastic-bodied car, in front of the Ford Engineering Laboratory in 1941.

Orville Wright, Charlie Taylor, and Henry Ford in the drafting room of the Ford Engineering Laboratory. Charlie Taylor was a mechanical genius and built the motor for the first engine powered airplane of the Wright Brothers.

1928 Model A Fordor Sedan in front of the Ford Engineering Laboratory.

A clay model prototype for a 1940 Lincoln Continental inside the
Ford Engineering Laboratory, July 1939.

A 1941 Ford Super DeLuxe Tudor.

Body Engineering prototype panel fitting at Ford Engineering Laboratory, 1946.

1942 Ford Super DeLuxe inside the Ford Engineering Laboratory.

Henry Ford, Albert Kahn, Mr. Martin, and Charles Sorenson at Ford Engineering Laboratory, circa 1942.

Aerial view of Ford Engineering Laboratory, 1946.

Engineering illustration of Sportsman wood body, 1946.

Clay modeling in the Ford Styling Studio at Ford Engineering Laboratory, 1946.

Checking clay dimensions in the Styling Studio at Ford Engineering Laboratory, 1946.

A clay model, 1938

Ford dynamometer test cell in Ford Engineering Laboratory, 1946.

The 1947 Ford Tudor Sedan.

Ford Engineering Laboratory, August 1951.

WRIGHT   BURBANK   EDISON   BURROUGHS   KIRBY   DI

Ford Engineering Laboratory, August 1951.

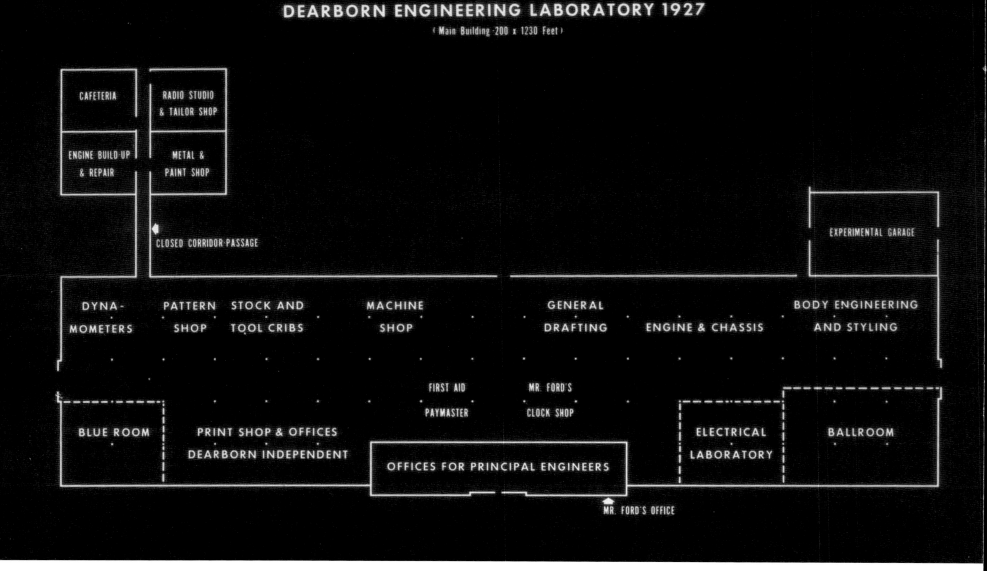

DEARBORN ENGINEERING LABORATORY 1927
(Main Building 200 x 1230 Feet)

CAFETERIA

RADIO STUDIO & TAILOR SHOP

ENGINE BUILD-UP & REPAIR

METAL & PAINT SHOP

CLOSED CORRIDOR PASSAGE

EXPERIMENTAL GARAGE

DYNA-MOMETERS

PATTERN SHOP

STOCK AND TOOL CRIBS

MACHINE SHOP

GENERAL DRAFTING

ENGINE & CHASSIS

BODY ENGINEERING AND STYLING

FIRST AID
PAYMASTER

MR. FORD'S
CLOCK SHOP

BLUE ROOM

PRINT SHOP & OFFICES
DEARBORN INDEPENDENT

ELECTRICAL
LABORATORY

BALLROOM

OFFICES FOR PRINCIPAL ENGINEERS

MR. FORD'S OFFICE

Above is a blueprint of the Ford Engineering Laboratory layout in 1927.

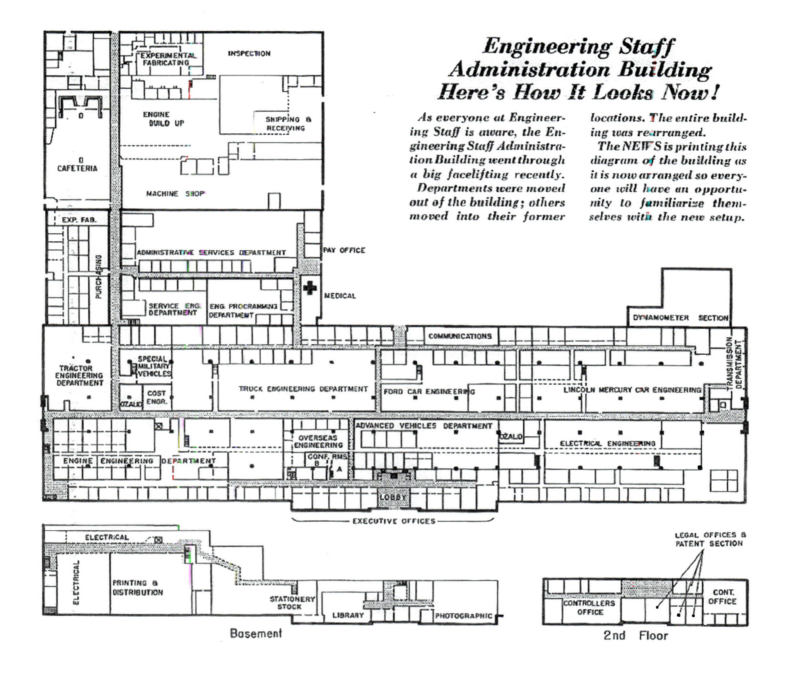

Engineering Staff Administration Building
Here's How It Looks Now!

As everyone at Engineering Staff is aware, the Engineering Staff Administration Building went through a big facelifting recently.

Departments were moved out of the building; others moved into their former locations. The entire building was rearranged.

The NEWS is printing this diagram of the building as it is now arranged so everyone will have an opportunity to familiarize themselves with the new setup.

In the early 1950's, the Ford Engineering Laboratory was known as the

Engineering Staff Administration building (ESA),

This is a floor plan from page 3 of the Ford Engineering Center News dated February 1953.

63

Henry Ford's office, circa 1924.

Henry Ford's office, circa 2007.

FRANKLINE

STOCKPOLE

Oct. 6 - 1938

W. CAMPBELL

C. E. SORENSEN

WIBEL

B. CRAIG

H. FORD

Mc. CARROL - E. FORD

MARTIN

SHELBRICK

In 1938, Mr. Ford, Edsel Ford and several other high-ranking managers marked their heights on one of the pillars holding up the roof. These marks were almost painted over in 1980 and are now protected with a brass frame.

During a period of bank mistrust the entire Ford cash payroll was located on the second floor of the POEE Building

The height chart of the 1938 management team is located on the north side of Pillar C10 in FEL. It is believed that this height chart was a means for understanding and determining headroom in Ford vehicles.

During an era of bank mistrust, Henry Ford stored payroll in this very large safe on the second floor of the Ford Engineering Laboratory.

This fireplace is in the library on the second floor of Ford Engineering Laboratory, located above Henry Ford's office.

One of two marble drinking fountains along Mahogany Row.

Henry Ford's office clock.

Aerial view of Ford Engineering Laboratory, now named
The Engine & Electrical Engineering (EEE) building, 1961.

The north side of the Ford Engineering Laboratory, 2015.

The Ford Engineering Laboratory showing its colors, undated.

The Ford Engineering Laboratory in winter, undated.

The Ford Engineering Laboratory in spring, undated.

Set In Stone

There are 21 names of scientists and inventors carved in the stone on the front of the Ford Engineering Laboratory building. These names were selected by Henry Ford and represent who he believed to have significantly contributed to advancing art and science for the service of mankind. He felt these names would inspire others who would fulfill similar ideals.

Charles Darwin- Scientist, formulated theory of natural selection

André Marie Ampère- Physicist, Mathematician, pioneer in electricity

Leonardo Da Vinci- Scientist, Artist, Engineer

Benjamin Franklin- Printer, Scientist, Statesman, made discoveries in electricity

Robert Fulton- Engineer, Inventor of a practical steamboat for passengers and freight

Eli Whitney- Industrial Pioneer, Inventor of the Cotton Gin

Alexander Graham Bell- Scientist, Inventor of the first practical telephone

Guglielmo Marconi- Scientist, Electrical Engineer, Inventor of the wireless telegraph

Orville Wright- Designer, Aeronautical Engineer father of aviation

Luther Burbank- Botanist, Inventor, pioneer in agricultural sciences

Thomas Alva Edison- Electrician, Inventor, known for the phonograph, incandescent lamp, kinescope

John Burroughs- Naturalist, Essayist

Frank E. Kirby- Naval Architect, Designer, Engineer of steamships, also former boss of Henry Ford

Rudolf Diesel- Mechanical Engineer, Inventor of the diesel engine

Michael Faraday- Scientist, Chemist, made important discoveries of magnetic induction

Mme. Marie S. Curie- Physicist, Chemist, discovered radium

Nikolaus Otto- Engineer, Inventor of the first practical 4-stroke internal combustion engine

Sir Isaac Newton- Physicist, Mathematician, formulated laws of gravitation and motion

Dr. John Boyd Dunlop- Veterinary Surgeon, Inventor, developed the first practical pneumatic tire

Louis Pasteur- Chemist, Microbiologist, pioneered work in vaccination and pasteurization

Galileo- Astronomer- Physicist, Philosopher, developed refracting telescope used to explore the universe, father of astronomy

At the center of the north end of the building there is a relief of a male and female figure seated on either side of a 1924 Ford Sedan. The male is holding an hourglass, which symbolizes the passing of time. He is also holding a pair of wings, a symbol associated with the Roman god Mercury, who is the patron of trade and commerce. The female is holding a cornucopia of gold coins and a caduceus, symbols of wealth and commerce. Between the figures is an abundant basket of fruit and atop sits an owl, which symbolizes wisdom. The relief suggests that the time for trade and commerce is now.

This relief shows a god representing communications as evidenced by his radio headset and the telegraph machine on the left. By 1910, wireless radio was a popular method of communications for business, government, and military. The lightning bolts symbolize electricity. Wireless communications work through electromagnetic signals.

This is located on the north end of the building.

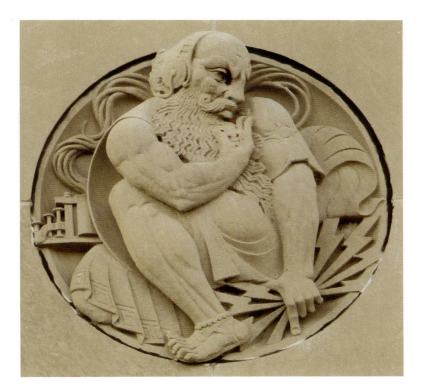

This figure represents transportation by sea. He holds in one hand a ship, which is powered by both wind and a motor as evidenced by the sails and the stack on the ship. He also is holding a scroll in his right hand that would symbolize a map.

This relief is also located on the north end of the building.

An Apothecary, or a man of medicine, is carefully combining ingredients. Behind him is a staff and the serpent, which is known as the rod of Asclepius, and is associated with healing or medicine. Medicine was very connected to agriculture and the growing of herbs and plants for health and wellbeing.

This relief is located on the west side of the building.

The god-like figure in this relief represents design, engineering, and architecture. Surrounding him are a compass, a plummet, and a scale. The scale has symbolic meaning, the weighted side representing the past, the fulcrum representing the present, and the non-weighed side, which is pointed upwards, is the future. Notice the tire treads in his hair and the needle bearing collar.

This relief is located on the west side of the building.

This relief shows a god-like figure with a peace pipe and a detonator. The peace pipe was used by Native Americans in peace talks. The detonator is used for new construction. This relief symbolizes peace and progress.

This is located on the west side of the building.

This very Romanesque god represents industry, specifically auto manufacturing, evidenced by the industrial stack behind him and the wheel he holds. His winged hat is also a symbol for trade and commerce.

This is located on the west side of the building.

Shown above is a decorative ornamental figure. There are two that are similar, on the front face of the building.

The Roman god Mercury was the god of trade, commerce, and transportation. This Romanesque figure represents mobility by trains. His winged hat is also the symbol for trade and commerce.

This is located on the west face of the building.

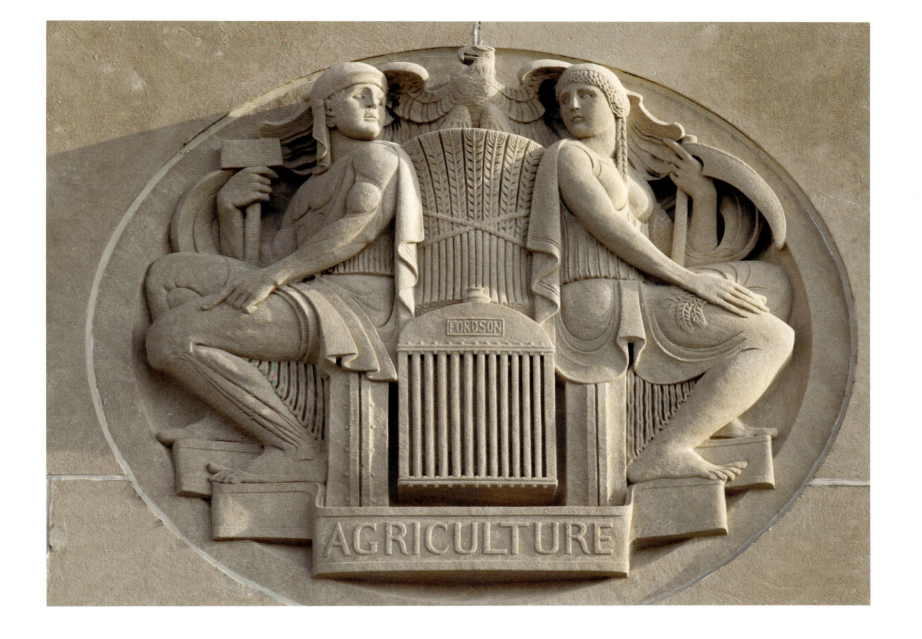

This relief is located on the south end of the building. It depicts a god and goddess of agriculture seated on either side of a Fordson tractor. The male is holding a hoe and the female is holding a large sickle, both implements of farming. Between them is a bale of wheat, and above the wheat is an eagle. This nicely represents American farmers.

This relief depicts a god-like figure holding a truck and a scepter, behind him is a curved roadway. The scepter is a symbol of a ruling monarch. This figure and his truck are rulers of the roads.

This is located on the west face of the building.

This is a Romanesque goddess of agriculture. She is shown here with a tractor and a hand sickle against the backdrop of wheat.

This is located on the south face of the building.

This relief represents agriculture. The figure is shown here with oxen, which would have been used to plow, and behind them grows a soybean plant. This relief is the only remaining relief on the east side of the original building. During a renovation in 1953, at least one relief on the east side of the building was covered.

This goddess represents flight, shown here with a plane, a bird perched on her shoulder and eagle in flight over a field of flowers below. This relief may very well represent Amelia Earhart, as she would have just set a world record for altitude in the fall of 1922. The cap on her head is a combination of a flight cap and a flapper's hat. Notice the stars and beads on the cap as well as the earring.

This is located on the south face of the building.

These are two similar, but different, Beaux-Art reliefs on the front facade of the building at either end. This one has a pair of gryphons facing one another. The gryphon is a mythical creature that combines the head of an eagle and the body of a lion. Gryphons are guardians of the divine. These two Gryphons appear to be guarding an eternal flame. An eternal flame was a way to remember soldiers particularly after the First World War.

This is located on the west face of the building.

This relief shows another pair of mythical creatures, winged lions. Winged lions protected the gates of Babylon. These lions are protecting an hourglass with a gear on top. The hourglass is a symbol of human life and the passage of time. The gear represents motion. The lions are protecting humanity as time moves forward.

This is located on the west face of the building.

The front, or west side, of the Ford Engineering Laboratory from the pond, 2015.

"To do for the world more than the world does for you—that is success.."

—Henry Ford

Index Of Photos

The following photos are from the collections of The Henry Ford Museum and Benson Ford Research Center:

All other photos are from the Ford Motor Company Archives.

IMPROVING LIVES. CURING TYPE 1 DIABETES.

Proceeds from this book will go to JDRF, the leading global organization funding type 1 diabetes (T1D) research. T1D is an autoimmune disease in which a person's pancreas stops producing insulin, a hormone that enables people to get energy from food. There is nothing you can do to prevent T1D, and—at present—nothing you can do to get rid of it. JDRF's mission is to accelerate life-changing breakthroughs to cure, prevent and treat T1D and its complications.

In 1998, under the leadership of Edsel B. Ford II, the Ford Global Action Team for JDRF was established. Since its inception, the employee-driven group has raised over $55 million in support of JDRF. No other company has done more to fund T1D research than Ford Motor Company.

Beth Ann Dalrymple is a Detroit native and a graduate of the University of Detroit Mercy. She works as a Thermal Fluid Analytical Engineer at Ford Motor Company. In 1990 she joined Ford's Engine Powertrain division and now works in Electrified Powertrain Engineering. One of her first jobs was working at the Willow Run Plant, another Henry Ford, and Albert Kahn collaboration. The Willow Run plant with its own historical significance in history during World War II is where her passion for industrial architecture and history began.

Raven Fields is a Graphic Designer and Communications Analyst for Ford Motor Company. After completing studies in the U.S. and Hong Kong, she earned her Bachelor of Fine Arts from Savannah College of Art and Design. As a fourth generation employee, she has enjoyed a strong connection to Ford's history. The Water Wheel Center, formally known as the Ford Valve Plant, was also designed by Albert Khan and remains a vibrant building in Raven's hometown of Northville, Michigan.